Carolyn White grew up in the kitchen. As a little helper, she measured salt and spices and soaked up her mom's recipes and flavor—fueling a lifelong love of cooking and entertaining. Although she loves elaborate dishes and testing new ideas on parishioners at Greater Works Baptist Church, her favorites are those she cooks up while friends are gathered around. And she often creates recipes to help her busy friends serve "gourmet" meals without a fuss. Outside of the kitchen, Carolyn is a licensed chemical dependency counselor and anger management therapist at Austin Recovery, a drug and alcohol treatment center. She lives in Austin, Texas, with her husband, Michael, who is her greatest supporter and her most avid taste-tester.

To order additional copies of this book, contact:
Xlibris Corporation
1-888-795-4274
www.Xlibris.com
Orders@Xlibris.com

# Special thanks to

Massalene White

Melissa Wolf

Stephanie Bosotik

Ollie Nickols

Kathy James

Michael White

# Pistachio Fried Chicken

**Ingredients**

1 whole chicken, cut up

1 tsp salt

1 tsp white pepper

¼ tsp curry powder

3 cups self-rising flour

½ tsp crushed red peppers

small jar Dijon mustard

1 tsp garlic powder

1 cup crushed pistachio

1 large red onion

peanut frying oil (oil of choice)

2 large eggs

2 ½ cup low-fat milk

large ziplock storage bags

**Direction**

Rinse chicken pieces, base with mustard, and season with salt, pepper (save some salt and pepper for mixture), and crushed peppers. Set aside. In a large bowl, mix eggs, milk, salt, and pepper together, and set aside. Mix flour, garlic powder, curry powder, and pistachios in a large ziplock storage bag. Rest several pieces of chicken in egg and milk mixture, let excess liquid drain, then place in flour bag, putting only a few pieces in mixture. In large pot heat oil (fill pot halfway, test oil with a pinch of flour to see if hot). Once oil is hot, cook a few pieces at a time. Continue this same process for the remaining pieces of chicken. Cook until golden brown and/or temperature reaches 360 degrees (or juices run clear, some pieces may take longer to cook depending on the size of chicken pieces). Rest hot chicken in bowl layered with paper towels to drain, slice onion, and scatter onion over cooked chicken. As chicken is being removed from hot oil, continue frying the rest of uncooked chicken. Serve hot. Five to six servings.

# Cream Cheese Corn Bread

**Ingredients**

1 box or bag corn bread mix

1 tbsp olive oil

3 tbsp flour

⅓cup condensed milk

4 tbsp 2% milk

¼ cup Philadelphia Whipped Cream Cheese

**Direction**

Preheat oven to 350 degrees. Follow the direction and ingredients on the back of corn bread package, add flour, add cream cheese, and both milk, and stir until mixture is creamy. In a small skillet, add olive oil and heat. Pour mixture into skillet and bake as directed on the back of corn bread package. Five to six servings.

# Glazed Salmon

### Ingredients

4 medium salmon steaks

pinch of salt

⅛ coarse black pepper

⅛ tsp minced garlic

3 tsp unsalted butter

1 small bag of pink cotton candy

1 package of hollandaise sauce (optional);
   cook as directed in package

### Direction

Season salmon on both sides with salt and pepper. In a medium saucepan, melt butter and garlic together, place salmon in skillet, skin down, and sear on each side for 4–5 minutes (or until salmon is pink inside or desired texture is achieved). Remove from heat, add 1 pinch of cotton candy, lay on top of each piece of salmon, cover, cook for another 1–2 minutes, remove from heating element, and serve. Four servings.

# Skewed Fruit Melody

**Ingredients**

1 apricot

1 lb of pineapples

2 large banana

5 kiwis

6 ounces semisweet chocolate

small container fresh strawberries

7 skewers

**Direction**

Cut fruit in medium chunks and place on a paper towel. Skew fruit diagonally onto skewers. Continuing process for the remaining of skewers. Melt chocolate according to instruction on jar. Spoon chocolate over fruit.

# Backyard Apple-Glazed Grill Chicken

**Ingredients**

1 split chicken

¼ cup honey-spicy mustard

½ cup brown sugar

⅓ cup apple juice (concentrated)

⅛ tsp salt

⅛ tsp coarse black pepper

large ziplock storage bag

**Direction**

Rinse and pat dry chicken, and place chicken on a flat and clean surface. Season chicken with salt and pepper, base chicken with mustard, and place in a large ziplock storage bag. Let rest in refrigerator for 1 hour. Add brown sugar and apple juice. Mix well and set aside. Remove chicken from refrigerator to reach room temperature. Heat grill (charcoal—wait until coals are white), place chicken on grill, brush on sauce, and cook for 10–15 minutes on each side before basing again. Continue to cook and base chicken, repeat until all chicken is done. Discard leftover basing.

Four to five servings.

# Garden Chicken Wrap

**Ingredients**

4 large chicken breast (boneless)

1 bottle zesty spicy Italian salad dressing

small bottle olive oil

⅛ tsp salt

⅛ tsp pepper

Boursin cheese

1 pint grape tomatoes

1 small bag baby spinach, remove stem

1 jar smoked peppers

1 large bell pepper

1 package flour tortillas

1 box large ziplock storage bags

**Direction**

Rinse and season chicken with salt and pepper. Pour salad dressing into a large ziplock storage bag (add chicken), and set in refrigerator for 1 hour. Heat grill (medium), remove chicken, and arrange chicken on grill. Cook for 5-7 minutes on each side or until chicken reaches 170 degrees. Rinse bell pepper, base bell pepper with olive oil, and place on grill rack for 5–7 minutes. Remove, slice and wrap bell pepper in foil. Place on grill to keep warm. Remove chicken, slice chicken in 4–5 slices, wrap in foil, and keep warm. Slice tomato and wash spinach, dry well, and tear into small pieces. Brush small amount of oil on tortilla, place on grill rack, and warm. Remove tortillas, spread cheese on warmed tortilla, and lay tomato, smoked peppers, bell peppers, and all fixings. Fold chicken in tortilla, cut diagonally, and serve. Four to five servings.

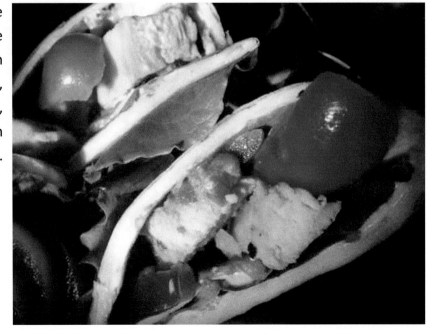

# Artichoke Steak Sandwich

**Ingredients**

3 medium-size rib eye steaks

1 lb prosciutto, sliced

salt and pepper (pinch)

1 medium artichoke, sliced

1 red onion

small bottle olive oil

2 bell peppers

6 slices provolone cheese

4 hoagie buns

1 large ziplock storage bag

**Direction**

Rinse and season steak with salt and pepper. Add all ingredients except artichoke and onions into a blender, and blend all coarse pieces until smooth. Pour mixture into a large ziplock storage bag, place steak into bag, place in refrigerator, and marinate for 2 hours. In medium nonstick skillet, heat of oil over medium heat, place steak in pan, sear on both sides to perfection. Remove steak from heat element, thinly slice & add prosciutto, cover in foil. Set aside. In the same steak pan, heat small amount of oil; add onions, bell peppers, and artichoke hearts; and sauté for 3–4 minutes. Remove steak from foil and slice steak into strips. Lay generous amount of steak and prosciutto mixture on top of heated bun and top with cheese and sauteed fixings. Three to four servings.

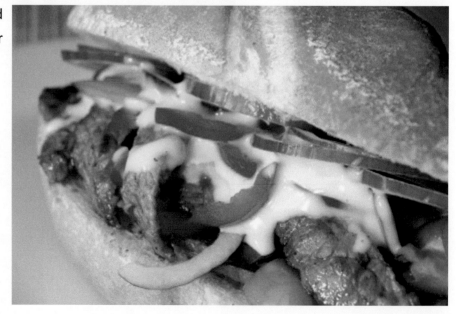

# Crunchy Banana Foster

## Ingredients

3 bananas

½ cup brown sugar

½ tsp cinnamon

1 cup honey-roasted pecan (pieces)

2 tsp butter

3 tbsp heavy cream

⅓ cup banana liqueur

½ tsp vanilla extract

4 scoops Spanish vanilla ice cream

½ pint dark rum

## Direction

In a medium-size saucepan over medium heat, add butter, cinnamon, and brown sugar. Stir until mixture is bubbly. Add vanilla extract, and stir in rum and banana liqueur (allowing liqueur to ignite). Stir in heavy cream, and continue to cook. Peel and cut bananas in half and place bananas in cream mixture. Cook until bananas are softened. Dip 1–2 scoops of ice cream and place in bowl; arrange banana pieces around ice cream. Spoon creamy mixture over ice cream, and sprinkle honey-roasted pecan pieces on top and serve. Four to five servings.

# Creamy Mac and Cheese Casserole

## Ingredients

8 oz elbow macaroni

2 tbsp butter

1 tsp salt

3 tbsp Philadelphia Cream Cheese

1 cup shredded cheddar

1 cup Monterey Jack Cheese

3 slices Roman bread

1 cup heavy cream

¼ cup Parmesan cheese, shredded

1 pint slim milk

olive oil cooking spray

## Direction

Preheat oven to 375 degrees. Follow direction on box to cook pasta adding salt, and butter. Meanwhile, using a toaster, toast bread to medium brown (if bread crumbs are not crunchy, place in oven and toast until flaky). Let cool. Crumb up bread, place in small bowl, add cheddar cheese, toss, and set aside. Remove pasta from heat element, drain, and slowly add all milk, cream cheese, cheddar, and Monterey Jack and Parmesan cheese, melt, and slightly fluff to mix in cheese ingredients. Spray casserole baking dish (9x13) with olive oil; pour cooked mac and cheese into baking dish, top with bread crumbs. Bake for 10 minutes or until cheese is melted. Four to five servings.

Carolyn White

# Scallop Potato Casserole

## Ingredients

5 large potatoes

1 cup heavy cream

1 cup 2% milk

⅓ tsp ginger

1 stick butter

2 ½ cups shredded cheddar and Monterey Jack
cheese (½ for casserole topping)

⅓ tsp salt

⅓ tsp pepper

1 box cheddar and chives box scallop potato (seasoning only)

parsley flakes (garnish)

paprika (garnish)

olive oil spray

## Direction

Heat oven to 350 degrees. Rinse and peel potatoes. Thinly slice potatoes (1 inch). Rinse again. Spray potatoes using olive oil spray, pour small amount of milk to bottom of baking dish, arrange one layer of potatoes in a large baking dish, sprinkle small amount of box potato seasoning, add salt, pepper, and ginger. Pour heavy cream, milk, 3–4 chunks butter (½ tablespoon in size), and cheese. Continue same process using all potatoes. Cover and bake for 1 hour or until tender (use fork to check for tenderness). Uncover sprinkle with remaining cheese and melt. Remove dish from oven, and garnish with parsley flakes and paprika.

# Garden Stuffed Chops

**Ingredients**

4 centered-cut pork chops (medium to thin cut)

1 8 oz sun-dried cream cheese

⅛ tsp salt

⅛ tsp pepper

3 tsp flour

⅓ cup olive oil

⅓ cup sherry wine

1 garlic powder

2 pieces pepper bacon

1 ½ cup fresh baby spinach

3 medium mushrooms, sliced

Red onion (chopped)

**Direction**

Preheat oven to 375 degrees. In a medium-size bowl, mix cream cheese and spinach together, and set aside. Rinse pork chops, cut a deep pocket in center of chops, season with salt, pepper, and garlic powder, and stuff. Heat olive oil in a small skillet over medium heat, sear both side of chops (save drippings), remove chops and place in a greased baking pan, cover, and place in oven for 30–40 minutes or until tender.

**Wine Sauce**

In the same skillet, fry bacon, onions, and mushrooms over medium heat. Stir in wine and simmer for 2–3 minutes. Stir in flour until liquid becomes smooth and simmer on low heat to cook in flour. Spoon sauce over plated pork chops.

# Moonlight Sausage Stick

**Ingredients**

5 smoked sausage links

5 skewers

1 red onion

1 red bell peppers

1 green bell peppers

2 large portabella mushroom

**Direction**

Soak skewers for approximately 5 minutes. Heat grill (indoors or outdoors) to medium heat. Slice sausage about 5 inches thick, and dice onions, both peppers, and mushrooms. Begin the skewing process starting with the mushroom, sausage (3), onions and peppers, mushrooms, and sausages. Continue skewing method until completion. Spray grill and place skewers on grill and grill for 10–15 minutes or to perfection. Remove from heat. Serve with favorite sides.

# Pesto Alla Genovese Chops

**Ingredients**

4 medium thick chops (bone in)

1 tsp ground pepper

1 tsp season salt

1 tsp minced garlic

2 tbsp alla Genovese pesto sauce

2 tbsp olive oil

1/3 cup parsley flakes

**Direction**

Garnish with parsley flakes. Rinse chops, and rub pesto sauce on chops and then season using dry seasoning. Under medium heat, heat oil in a grill pan grill chops on each side for 7-8 minutes or until chops are no longer pink inside.

# Tequila Grilled Chicken Breast

## Ingredients

4 skinless boneless chicken breast

½ cup chopped red onion

1 cup chopped celery

¼ cup olive oil

¼ cup tequila

⅓ cup minced garlic

salt (pinch)

1 tsp pepper

⅓ cup Italian salad dressing

⅓ crushed red pepper

¼ jalapeno seasoning salt

olive grill spray

## Direction

Rinse chicken breast and rest breast on paper towel. Place onion, celery, garlic, Italian dressing, olive oil, and tequila in a processor and blend until smooth. Pour mixture into a large food storage bag, place chicken into food bag, and refrigerate for 2.5 hours. Preheat gas grill to medium high. Remove chicken breasts from marinade. Sprinkle remaining seasoning, spray grill, and grill over medium high heat for 4 to 5 minutes on each side. Make sure chicken is cooked through by checking for juices to run clear. Three to four servings.

# Beef Tenderloin

**Ingredients**

4 tenderloin steaks

¼ tsp garlic salt

⅛ tsp pepper

2 tbsp olive oil

3 cloves garlic (peeled; sliced thin)

Dijon mustard

1 10 oz bag wild mushroom garlic herb sauce

1 beef bouillon

1/3 cup sherry wine

**Direction**

Rinse steak. Base steak with mustard and season with garlic salt and pepper. In a saucepan over medium heat, add olive oil and garlic and saute for 3-4 minutes. Place steak into pan and sear on both side, add wine and continue simmering to desire texture (145 medium & 160/170 well done). In a different pan heat sauce according to directions on bag then add bouillon then simmer. Spoon sauce over steak.

# Roasted Pepper Shrimp Pasta

## Ingredients

15–20 jumbo shrimp (deveined and peeled)

3 cups fresh spinach

6 cups fettuccine pasta

⅛ tsp salt

1 ½ stick butter

8 cloves garlic, thinly sliced

1 cup heavy cream

1 bottle white wine

1 cup green bell pepper (thinly sliced)

1 cup red bell pepper (thinly sliced)

1 ⅓ cup fresh Parmesan cheese, grated

¼ tsp olive oil

1 ½ cups wild mushrooms (sliced)

1 10 oz jar tapenade roasted red peppers

1 15 oz jar Bertolli Alfredo sauce

## Direction

Set at medium heat. Prepare pasta in large pot of water and wine, add salt and ½ of the garlic, and use equal amount of water and wine as directed on package. Set aside. Rinse, drain, and pour olive oil over pasta and toss for even coating. Set aside. Rinse spinach and let drain or pat dry using paper towels. Set aside. Rinse shrimps, and set aside. In large saucepan add mushrooms, remaining garlic, peppers, butter, and melt. Arrange shrimps in pan and sauté until translucent. Once sautéed, add pasta sauce and roasted red peppers. Reduce heat, and simmer for 10 minutes. Add heavy cream and spinach and simmer for another 3 minutes to combine all seasoning. Add pasta to mixture, and fold pasta into mixture. Sprinkle grated cheese on top. Four to five servings.

# Garlic Smashed Potatoes

**Ingredients**

6 medium peeled Idaho potatoes

1 tsp salt

⅛ tsp pepper

½ cup heavy cream

3–4 tbsp unsalted butter

1 8 oz Boursin garlic cream cheese

fresh parsley flakes (garnish)

**Direction**

Set at medium heat. Bring water to a boil. Add potatoes and salt. Cook until potatoes are tender. Drain potatoes, and add cream cheese, pepper, and butter. Use a potato masher or large fork to smash potatoes, and stir in heavy cream. Sprinkle parsley flakes on top. Three to four servings.

# Chipotle Cheeseburger

**Ingredients**

1 lb ground meat

⅛ tsp pepper

2 tbsp chipotle mustard

3 tbsp A1 steak sauce

red onions, sliced

1 bag spring salad mix

tomatoes, sliced

6 slices pepper bacon

4 bakery hamburger buns

4 slices provolone cheese

olive oil mayo

1 can Omega 3 pan spray

**Directions:**

Preheat stove top grill for medium heat. Slightly rinse meat. Place ground meat in a large mixing bowl, combine top four ingredients, and mix well. Make patties to desired size, and spray grill with omega olive oil grill spray. Grill for 7–8 minutes. Turn and cook other side to perfection. Grill bacon until done, and set aside. Place bun on grill, heat, and remove bun. Top patties with cheese during the last few minutes of grilling. Assemble burger using burger fixings. 4 servings.

# Braised Short Ribs

**Ingredients**

6-8 short rib

1 cup chopped celery

1 red onion

3 tsp course black pepper

1/3 tbsp grape seed or olive oil

3 tsp jalapeno seasoning

1tbsp butter

1 can chipotle peppers

1tsp brown sugar

3 tbsp mustard

3 tsp salt

**Direction**

Rinse beef. Add oil to pan and heat. Season beef with jalapeno seasoning, pinch of salt and pepper and sear on both sides. Add celery and onions. Cover and cook for 25-30 minutes on top of stove. Remove top and pour down drippings. Add butter, chipotle peppers, mustard and brown sugar to beef, cover and place in oven and cook for 40-45 minutes or until tender. Three to four servings.

Printed in the United States
by Baker & Taylor Publisher Services